You Are Here for a
PURPOSE

Living Life to the Fullest in All Seasons

VANYA KOEPKE

Trilogy Christian Publishers
A Wholly Owned Subsidary of Trinity Broadcasting Network
2442 Michelle Drive
Tustin, CA 92780

For information, address Trilogy Christian Publishing
Rights Department, 2442 Michelle Drive, Tustin, CA 92780.
Trilogy Christian Publishing/TBN and colophon are trademarks of
Trinity Broadcasting Network.
For information about special discounts for bulk purchases, please
contact Trilogy Christian Publishing.
Manufactured in the United States of America

10 9 8 7 6 5 4 3 2 1
Library of Congress Cataloging-in-Publication Data is available.
ISBN 979-8-88738-938-7
ISBN 979-8-88738-939-4 (ebook)

Table of Contents

Foreword
by Mayor Jim Schmitt

There are many special people in this world, and as the longest serving mayor in Green Bay's history, I have had the pleasure of meeting many of them—from presidents to movie stars, businesswomen to community leaders, and of course many athletes, especially those who've played for the Green Bay Packers. But I can honestly say that one of the most genuine and impressive people I've met over the course of my lifetime is Vanya Koepke. Anyone who has met Vanya knows that he has a good heart and the innate ability to uplift all of those around him. As this book will show, Vanya experienced a unique set of circumstances and challenges that many people cannot imagine, and yet through his resilience, hard work, and belief in himself and his faith, he has achieved wonderful successes and bettered the lives of those in his community. His positivity and genuine heart are things he has been intentional about and worked towards.

I was fortunate to meet Vanya when he was president of the student government at the University of Wisconsin-Green Bay. Even as a young college student, I could sense his desire and purpose to do good things. Vanya worked for me in the mayor's office as an intern, dealing with the wide breadth of challenges and opportunities a city faces day in and day out. He would meet with many of our residents, each person different in age, background, and their reason for coming to city hall, and yet everyone—I mean everyone, found Vanya to be sincere, compassionate, and concerned for their wellbeing and the overall success of our community.

Vanya truly lives his faith, and his willingness to share his story is an act of generosity and another way in which he aims to uplift those he encounters in life. Our world can often be one made up of struggles and setbacks, but in reading Vanya's story and perspective we can all take comfort that we are indeed here for a purpose.

I am proud of Vanya's accomplishments, and I have the utmost belief that with his strong faith and ability to find the good in even the toughest situations, Vanya will continue to do great things for all of us and the good of all God's people. Let his story be a lesson in empathy, hard work, and all that can be achieved when a person is driven to make a difference.

Acknowledgment and Prayer

I would like to dedicate this book to you, the reader, with the hope and prayer that it impacts your life in a positive way.

I would also like to say thank you to my amazing wife Callee, and to our families, my parents, and all those who helped me to put this book together. Your love, support, and encouragement mean so much.

I would also like to give all the glory to God—and my Lord and Savior Jesus Christ. He is the Author of your story and deserves all the praise.

Lastly, my prayer is this: "Dear God, please meet the readers of this book where they are. Give them a stillness and a focus to hear from You as they read these words. Give them the resolve to make any necessary changes in their lives and not let the words they read fade away. Encourage them if they need encouragement, challenge them if they need to be challenged, even irritate them if needed, but ultimately give them a vision for their purpose in life and help them to be a little different at the end of the book. Don't leave us the same, God. Amen."

Introduction

Have you ever wondered what your purpose in life is? How can you live the most fulfilling life? Why should the worst of failures and the grandest successes not define you? What is your purpose as a leader (or a follower— we don't all have to be leaders and need more books on following the right leaders/leadership styles)? A single parent? As a grandparent, or as a boss? What is my purpose as someone currently thriving or someone who is currently struggling?

These are just a few of the questions that most of us may have wrestled with at some point. In turn, the goal of this book is to share my life experiences and connect moments of pain, failure, and success to finding purpose in God; more specifically, a personal relationship with Jesus Christ. Now, if you are looking for a faith book, excellent! If you are not, don't close this book after one paragraph. I encourage you to keep reading, as these stories will meet you where you are and do not aim to convert you towards faith, but rather encourage you to put life into the perspective of pursuing your purpose. If you find faith or already believe, that is just a bonus!

As you may have noted, the subtitle of this book is *Living Life to the Fullest in All Seasons*. This subtitle is focused on equipping you with the necessary tools to live out the purpose for which you were designed, no matter what life may throw your way. I also describe how my parents' leap of faith transformed my life story. In turn, may my story allow you to reflect on your story and see your worth and purpose in all seasons of life.

While this book does not identify your specific purpose (as only you can do that), it does aim to keep you on the path of a purpose-driven life (no matter how often you may fall off this path). Further, may this book help you take stock of your life, reflect, and find a friend or a mentor to help you identify and live out your purpose, not alone but in community. This book will also remind or inform you that you are not an accident; your life is not a series of coincidences, you are redeemed (made new), and that your life is about something bigger than you. As you will see, I have found my purpose to be one of loving God, living for God, and helping people in my life. I am choosing daily to not be a people pleaser, but a God pleaser. I am choosing to live out Matthew 6:33, "But seek first his kingdom and his righteousness, and all these things will be given to you as well."

Growing up, my family would often print off MapQuest driving directions for any basketball trips or vacations. Yes, such technology points to a time when we didn't use paper maps but before today's technology of free smartphone Google Maps directions. Nonetheless, the MapQuest form of directions allowed us to reach our destination. MapQuest was our trip compass. In turn, when we look deeper into the title of this book, we will see that what you make the foundation of your life will ultimately be the compass to your purpose. This compass must not be left behind at home (but rather taken with you on the journey of life), the compass must be followed, and the compass must be reviewed for accuracy to make sure you are staying on the correct path (and will reach the desired destination). Similarly, once discovered, your purpose should not be left behind. Your purpose should guide you. Lastly, you should take stock and review the direction in which the compass is taking you. In all, the key points of this book include:

Discovering your purpose through vulnerability.

Living your purpose in all seasons of life.

Living your purpose through genuine relationships.

Reflecting on your purpose through humility.

Redirecting your purpose based on your source of truth.

In connection with these key points, I have created a diagram for your reference. As you review the diagram in the next chapter, consider how the diagram may look in your life. What do you have inserted in each block? Some of these blocks will have a chapter dedicated to them, while others will be woven throughout the book. This diagram is based on my life and what I have experienced, and should be used as a guide, rather than exact science when considering the pursuit of your purpose.

My hope and prayer are that this book both reawakens your faith and inspires you to live out your purpose to the fullest.

The Building Blocks in Pursuit of Purpose

What is life? Why are we here? What is our purpose? Just a few light thoughts we might have on our lunch break. While it may be funny, or something you haven't thought of (specifically at lunch), life, purpose, belonging and relationships certainly cross our minds at some point. In fact, I would argue that life comes down to the two ideas of *purpose* and *relationships*. We all want to have a purpose. We all want to contribute to our lives and the lives of those around us. We also desire relationships. Whether belonging to a community, a significant other, family, friends, or company—relationships matter. We truly seek purpose and relationships as the foundation of all we do. Are you living for money? Are you living for hard work? Are you living for a promotion? Well, these become your purpose. Are you living to be popular? Are you living to be included? Are you living for family, friends, or significant others? Well, these become your relationships. You can also mix and match these and other areas to identify your current purpose. In and of themselves, these things are not bad or evil.

However, if these areas of your life stand alone, with no foundation, then the challenge we face is that of unfulfillment and disappointment.

In turn, let's dive into the next chapters, and reflect on what our purpose here on earth may be. As the title of this book says, you are here for a purpose. No matter the challenges or successes you have had in the past, the challenges or successes you are going through now, or the challenges/successes you will have, all of those experiences are leading to your fullest potential, purpose, and ultimately the way you impact the relationships around you. Consider the following diagram as an outline for what this book is all about. What do you currently have inserted in each block? What change is needed?

Purpose		
Definitions	Preferences	Humility
Vulnerability	Genuine Relationships	Decision-Making
Source of Truth		

Source of Truth: is the foundation and compass to the pursuit of your purpose.

Vulnerability: is your new strength in your pursuit of purpose.

Genuine Relationships: are your guardrails as you pursue your purpose.

Decision-Making: is your confidence and reassurance in pursuit of your purpose.

Definitions: are your guide to being consistent with your source of truth in pursuit of your purpose.

Preferences: are your second guide to being consistent with your source of truth in pursuit of your purpose.

Humility: is your cornerstone and mirror that allows you to reflect, measure progress and redirect as needed in pursuit of your purpose.

Purpose: is you living out your source of truth and the other building blocks to the fullest with enjoyment. You must roll up your sleeves and get after it!

Before we proceed, I would like to cover the blocks of definitions and preferences in greater detail, as I will not dedicate extensive time to them throughout the book. As mentioned earlier, definitions and preferences are your guides to consistent habits. Further, if your source of truth/compass is properly aligned, and you are following its guidance, then how you define and interpret events around you will be consistent with your source of truth and ultimately your purpose. Similar to definitions, the way you create and live out personal preferences should be consistent with your source of truth. After all, how inconsistent is it to have preferences that do not line up with your definitions or source of truth? For instance, if your source of truth (the foundation of the diagram) is academia, but instead of reading, writing, and researching, you only watch Netflix, then your definitions and preferences are not consistent with your source of truth. Similarly, if like me, your source of truth/compass is Christianity (loving God, loving people, and a personal relationship with Jesus), but instead of reading the Bible, attending church, and living out your faith in action, you define and prefer to have your faith be something else, or the exact opposite, then there is again a lack of consistency with the source of truth. Like any source of truth, Christianity has uncompromisable definitions such as the Bible being God's inspired word and Jesus being the Son of God. At the same time, preferences for a style of music in the church, a denomination choice, or the light settings in the church, are simply preferences that are neither right nor wrong, and can be chosen while staying consistent to the core of Christianity. Lastly, you can pick and choose how preferences and definitions guide your voting, schooling options, and many other areas. The combinations are numerous, but if you are honest with yourself, you will know if preferences and definitions are truly guiding you to consistency with your source of truth.

At this point it is important to reflect on why I did not make a case for identity when considering your purpose. After all, when you look at the definition of purpose and identity you see unique definitions. Purpose is defined as: "the reason for which something is done or created, or for which something exists," while identity is defined as: "the fact of being who or what a person or thing is." The reason as to why I did not focus on identity is because our society is overwhelmed with this focus. Whether celebrities, influencers, or social media, too much focus has been made on finding yourself—your identity. Whether finding oneself through a sexual identity, an academic identity, or a faith identity, we must see that identity is helpful, but is ultimately selfish.

When we spend so much time focused on ourselves, we lose ourselves and our purpose along the way.

While it is good to have a general idea of who we are (identity), it is not necessary to overanalyze our identity. This is the case, as I believe the more invested we are in a solid foundation of our lives, the better we will know who we are. Furthermore, we will have more opportunities for our purpose and helping those around us. Are self-reflections and self-care helpful? To an extent, yes, however, life is very short and if we want to live out our purpose to the fullest in all seasons, we must heavily invest in the right foundation and the source of truth in our lives. We must be purpose-driven, rather than identity-driven. This world needs more of "we" and less of "me." A focus on our purpose puts down the barriers of phones, ear pods, lack of eye contact, and opens our minds to things and opportunities so much bigger than our identities. We now see our purpose through a clearer lens.

You Are Not an Accident, a Coincidence, or a Mistake

Born in Tomsk, Russia on May 22nd, 1992, a healthy baby boy, Ivan Genadevich Bezhenzev's future looked promising. Ivan was supposed to be a child of a Russian naval officer, living a middle-class lifestyle, and pursuing the orchestra aspirations of his father, as well as the organizational abilities of his mother. Surrounded by three uncles, two aunts named Luba (translated to mean love), cousins, and two half-sisters, his heart was supposed to be filled with love, overwhelming care, and honesty for those around him.

Yet Ivan's utopian future was not to be. While born as a healthy, ten-pound baby, his left collarbone had to be broken during birth to get him out. Shortly before turning two, Ivan was hospitalized with a severe cold that almost killed him. Ivan was also the son of a former naval officer with severe PTSD, whose escape from life was alcohol and who was no longer a clean and well-put together man.

I will not prolong this story too much before saying that this was my real-life story. Named after my great-grandpa who was affectionately called Vanya, I have always been called Vanya rather than the formal name of Ivan. Prior to my birth, my biological father was involved in a submarine accident. After a malfunction, the submarine was submerged for hours while losing oxygen, leading to the death of twenty-seven of the thirty men on board. My father witnessed one of them pulling out a pistol and committing suicide. Only my father and two of his crew members survived. This unfortunate event led to my father's PTSD and his wife leaving him with their two daughters (my now half-sisters, Lena and Tatiana). A few years later my father, Genadevich Alexsandrovich Bezhenzev, who was born on December 20th, 1939, met my biological mom, Zinaida Aleksevna Holodova, and shortly afterwards I was born. My father was fifty-three and mother was forty-four when they had me. The likelihood of my birth kept defying the odds.

Growing up with two disengaged parents was not easy. From what I recall—and according to my father's younger sister Aunt Luba—she would often find me unfed and unchanged in my crib, but almost always smiling and sitting contently in my mess. Thanks to my aunt and neighbors, I was cared for, fed, and given as much support as they could give. Still, these experiences were the birthplace of the pain I would carry for years to come.

At the age of three I went to recycle some glass bottles with my biological dad to make some money as we were poor. When we left, I still have vivid images of my biological mom standing on a chair, painting the ceiling. When we came back to the house, my mom was lying lifeless on the ground in a pool of white paint. I would later learn that she died of a heart attack—she was only forty-seven years old. For a woman born on March 14th of 1948, her life was truly cut too short.

With my father's PTSD, the added stress of losing his partner (he and my biological mother were not married), only added to my loss of a present father. Between the ages of three and five, I would often walk the streets of my neighborhood asking for food. At the time, thanks to the generosity and hospitality of my neighbors, in my mind I was simply asking for help. Still, as I reflect on the situation years later, I was begging for food to get by for most of those two years. On the good days, my Aunt Luba and other extended family would bring food and watch me. There were also instances where my dad would leave with his buddies to go drinking, and his buddies' kids would lock me in a room or the pigeon house (my dad raised pigeons as a hobby) and run away. I once got out and climbed on a stacked pile of logs at least 10 feet high, when I slipped and fell. Somehow, I got out of that fall with no major injuries. However, I took it all in stride and made the most of each situation. If locked in the house, I would start sweeping, cleaning, and putting things in order. I thought that no matter how chaotic life was around me, I could still create order. Aunt Luba and Grandma Poluferia recall the times they were over at the house and asked me to clean up my toys. I would not only put away my toys, but pick up a broom and sweep the area I played in. After seeing what alcohol did to my biological dad, I have refused to drink.

Did you know that some of our best habits may form out of a challenge?

Shortly after turning five, my Aunt Luba and Uncle Vitya explored adopting me. However, they were not approved by the Russian government due to the financial obligation I would bring in addition to having to raise their own two daughters. In turn, I was placed in an orphanage and was allowed to have family visits and to stay with my aunts and uncles on weekends and holidays. The support system of my extended family aided me in being better behaved than most kids at the orphanage and allowed me to be a more adoptable child. While I was pleasant, I was not bilingual (I knew not a word of another language) and this would only add to the strain of me being adopted, as perhaps I could not connect with the host families well. I was also a stubborn and sassy orphan kid who would at times disobey my teachers, tease my classmates, and get into trouble. Most of the time the punishment for these actions was a time-out, a mandatory nap (ohh how I wish this is how adults got punished today), a spanking with a rubber slipper, and on one occasion (when I was extra sassy), a whipping with poison ivy. I remember the poison ivy incident clearly. I was at the orphanage summer camp, did not follow instructions, and started teasing my teacher by jumping on the top bunk beds to get away from her. The room was a square, so I was able to keep up the act for a bit, but she eventually got me, and it did not go over so well. To this day, I know exactly what poison ivy looks like and always remind myself and those with me to stay away from it.

At the age of six, I was selected to stay for a month with a host family in Spain. In this system, if the family liked their hosted child, after a month they could pursue adoption. After an enjoyable month in Spain, I never heard back from the host family. Given the language barrier, I also did not understand whether the family truly liked me while I was there. I did wonder if they did not adopt me because I once locked the host mom in the bathroom. While the pain and insecurity of not living with a family in Russia or not being wanted with a family in Spain grew, I knew that if I pushed down the hurt and put on a happy face, I may one day be loved and accepted into a family.

Two years later, I was selected to stay with a host family in Long Island, New York. At the age of eight, the hope of being part of a family was rekindled, but as with the previous host experience, this one would only leave me disappointed. After a month in New York, I came back to the orphanage with no word from the family (more to come about my experience in New York and what all happened). Let me say that I was a bitter, insecure, and a prideful child after these experiences. All I wanted was to be loved and accepted. I wanted to find meaning and a purpose. I wanted a family. I may have not known it then, but the future of most Russian orphanage kids at eighteen was $300 of Social Security money, one year of mandatory military service, and most likely an overdose death on the streets shortly thereafter. I know that my situation may not have been as dire as fellow orphans who truly had no one outside the orphanage; however, I was just a kid who wanted acceptance, love, and a family. Little did I know that once again, two years later, a family was looking for a child to adopt. The start of the next chapter will be written from the perspective of my mother, Dawn Koepke.

Even Our Best Plans
Have a Better Planner

Mom: "We started the adoption process in January of 2002. We were hoping to adopt a girl aged 4-6 and one boy 6-8 years old. We had gone back and forth about which country to adopt from, Ukraine or Russia. After many things like the fact that Paul's dad knew some Russian, Paul's cousin had just married a Russian woman, there were more children available, we loved the culture, and the history has always interested me, we both agreed and decided on Russia.

"The process began with the home study, where we were interviewed by a social worker. She came out to meet our kids and see our home and yard and do background checks on us. We had to get four letters of reference from friends and our pastor. We also had to write a several page biography for each of us, plus a lot of other paperwork. Once the home study was completed and approved, then we started the pre-dossier paperwork that would be sent to Russia to get things going there. This paperwork included a police check, abuse/ neglect check, employer verification, and pictures of us. This paperwork, along with all the home study information, helped them get to know us. This paperwork got the ball rolling on the search for potential children.

"We then started our dossier paperwork that was some of the same stuff we had already done and some more in-depth information on us, our financial standing, etc. This work had to be complete for parents to receive an invitation to travel to Russia and meet potential children. When we were on the tail end of finishing this paperwork, we received a call saying they had some videos/pictures and medical information of two children for us to look over. We were very surprised, because we were told most regions were not sending anything before you traveled anymore; you had to go to Russia and meet a child and choose one there.

"The first videos we saw were of a five-year-old boy, whom we later met at Galina's orphanage, and an 8-year-old girl named Svetlana. After watching the boy's video, we knew that he was not the right boy for our family, and also not the age we were looking for. Svetlana, too, was not the girl the Lord had for our family. Shortly after, we were sent two more videos. One of them was Galina's and the other a boy named Peter, from your orphanage. After viewing these videos and sending them to an international adoption doctor for viewing, we decided to commit to these two children. Little did we know that God had other plans for us.

"More paperwork followed (always paperwork), and they told us that we would probably be traveling to pick up our children mid-October. We started getting things ready, like buying clothes, winter outerwear, and boots, getting the rooms ready, and doing a lot of reading. The first week in October we got our call that we could travel to Russia, and we had six days to get there! One other thing: Laws had changed, and they required us to travel twice now. We would meet our kids on the first trip, leave, and come back at a later date for court and to bring the children home. We were so disappointed. We were ready to bring our kids home. Plus, we had worked so hard to get all the money together, and this would cost us another $7,000-$10,000. We worried about the weekend away and tried to figure out what to do. We called our agency Monday morning and told them that we would only be able to adopt one of the children, and since we had more information on Galina, we decided to only adopt her.

"As the week progressed, we really didn't feel any peace about our decision. We felt that we were lacking faith. God had provided all the money so far; we needed to trust that He would continue to take care of us. So, we called the agency back again to tell them that we had changed our minds, again, and that we would adopt both children. The day before we were to travel, our agency called us with more bad news. After we had called to say we could not adopt Peter, the orphanage had found another family for him. If we still wanted to adopt another little boy, we could meet one there. Again, we were very disappointed, but God was in control.

"Paul, Tyler, and I boarded our plane in Chicago and started our trip to Russia. Our trip to Moscow and then on to Tomsk went very smoothly. We were so excited to see what God would do. When we got to Tomsk, it was freezing and snowing. I couldn't believe there was snow in October. Our translator was there to pick us up, and we were taken to our hotel to get some sleep and then we would visit Galina's orphanage first. We were so excited that we couldn't sleep at all.

"We went to meet Galina that day. After our visit, our translator asked us if we were still considering adopting a second child. If we were, there were two boys we could meet at another orphanage the next day. So, the next day, after visiting Galina, we drove to your orphanage. It was way bigger than Galina's. Your orphanage had about 150-200 kids in it ranging from 6-16. We were taken to the social worker's office and spent some time talking with her. Then they brought you in.

"They had told us that you were a healthy 10-year-old boy who liked basketball and swimming and was very smart and artistic. You were a little older than what we had first decided on, but we wanted to be open to whatever God wanted for our family. My first impression of you was that you were very handsome and smart, but somewhat defensive. You seemed a little nervous or scared, and I didn't blame you. I was told to ask you a question. I asked questions about your schooling, interests, and friends; how long you had lived in the orphanage, and a host of other questions. You answered every question quickly and confidently. When I ran out of questions, they dismissed you from the room, and we went over your medical information. Then they asked us if we wanted to meet the other boy. Much to their surprise, we told them no, that we wanted to make a decision about you first.

"That evening, we talked about our meeting with you, and we all agreed that we wanted you to be part of our family. We were so glad that Tyler had come along, because we were worried that you were too close to his age, and that it might bother him. He was sure that he, too, wanted you to be part of our family.

"We were only able to visit you a couple more times before we had to leave to go back home. We gave you a few gifts and a photo album and talked to you about why we had to leave, but that we would be back in a few weeks. As we left, you kissed me on the cheek and called me Mama. As I sat in the car on the way home, tears filled my eyes. We had been so disappointed and angry that a second trip had been added, but if it hadn't, we would never have had the opportunity to adopt you. I am so glad God knows what is best, and He knew you were best for our family! Ya tibya loobloo, Vanya, moy sin!" (Galina and I would be officially adopted on November 27th, 2002).

As I read my mom's adoption experience, I can't help but tear up and reflect fully on how much I love my parents for what they did, but also thank God for His faithful planning. After all, it would have been easy for my parents to give up when their adoption plans did not work out. Yet, my parents did not give up. They lived out Jeremiah 29:11, "'For I know the plans I have for you,' declares the Lord, 'plans to prosper you and not to harm you, plans to give you hope and a future.'" My parents also lived out Joshua 1:9 (a verse I have by my and Callee's front door today), "Be strong and courageous. Do not be afraid; do not be discouraged, for the Lord your God will be with you wherever you go." Mom and Dad had to choose to not rely on their plans, but to trust the plans of God, our perfect Planner. As you reflect on your plans, which old, recent, or future plans have failed you or which may you have to choose to let go of? Your plans may be closely related to my parents' story, or entirely different. Still, as you consider your plans, who truly owns those plans? Do you own the plans, or do you allow God to have ownership of your plans? If my parents had not been flexible with what the Master Planner was about to do, I would not be in America, be part of an amazing family, nor be writing this book. In turn, consider the following:

- What is the purpose of your plan?
- Who owns your plan?

- Who will benefit from your plan?
- Are you flexible (to the point of surrender) with your plan?

These questions are a crucial foundation towards reaching your purpose. In fact, the answers to these questions will either hold you back or allow you to take the next step in reaching your purpose.

My encouragement to you is to live a life of surrendered plans, as plans that are surrendered to God will allow for your purpose to flourish.

While I may never know why I was not adopted in Spain, I did find out why I was not adopted by the New York host family. At 17, I was looking through the photo album my host family had given me. I noticed their address and phone number on the first page of the album. Though it had been nine years since I was with them, I decided to call the number. Thinking that they most likely had moved or the number did not work, I had low expectations for the call. However, the phone was picked up, and I heard, "Hi, this is Liz." My introduction of "Hi, this is Vanya" was met with slight confusion, so I cleared it up and reintroduced myself as Ivan (the name my host family used). From there, there were a few tears, a few laughs, some disbelief and a few more tears as I spoke with Kevin and Elizabeth for almost an hour. As I informed them that I had been adopted seven years earlier and was living with my family in Wisconsin, they were relieved and said that they were in the process of adopting me themselves shortly after my stay with them. However, due to some health issues on their end, they would not be able to resume the process until two years later when I was ten and had just been adopted. In all, this new East Coast family connection gave me closure from the past and has allowed for a beautiful friendship to form. I have visited Kevin and Elizabeth a few times in New York since, as well as hosting them for a Packers game (and overtime win against the Bengals) in Wisconsin.

Remember, your life is not an accident. Events in your life are not a coincidence. You are not a mistake. Your mistakes do not define you. Know that your current circumstances may not reveal the very best that lies ahead for you. After all, my adoption story was not a coincidence or a lucky roll of the dice. My adoption story went from impossible—given that my friend Peter was the first in line—to unlikely, when my parents were leaning to only adopt Galina, to now seeing God's perfect plan and will for my life and ultimately the lives of those around me. Did you know that Peter lived on the left side of the orphanage, on the third story, in a room on the right side, where there were twenty kids? It still amazes me today that the next batch of DVDs and adoption files that my parents got came from the right side of the orphanage, on the second story, in the room on the right with another twenty of the 200 kids in the orphanage. That DVD and adoption file was mine, and God was clearly telling my parents, "No more messing around; the third time is the charm." God uses our doubt for His purposes. Whether changing minds about pursuing the adoption of two kids instead of one, or changing our minds about our belief and surrender to Christ, He uses it all. As God did with my parents and my adoption story, He too can do it with you—amidst any circumstances you are facing.

Stay in community, stay focused, and choose to see the bigger picture. Your purpose can start with the surrender of your plans.

Your Purpose
through the Valleys

Since accepting Jesus as my Lord and Savior at the age of twelve, I have often been reminded that not only do we choose God, but God chooses to accept us daily. These reminders have come to me through my most trying moments.

A month before my seventeenth birthday, my parents helped me organize a trip back to Russia for the first time since being adopted. I was excited to see my Russian family for a few reasons. First was the company of my extended family and their amazing food. Second was because I had felt led to share my faith with my elderly biological father. After a thirteen-hour flight from Chicago to Moscow, a ten-hour layover in Moscow, and another four-hour flight from Moscow to my hometown, Tomsk, I finally reconnected with my Aunt Luba and Uncle Vitya. My aunt and uncle have been my God-sent angels since birth. They were there for me consistently from birth until I was five and in the poor custody of my biological parents. Aunt Luba's and Uncle Vitya's visits to the house were extremely beneficial for me, as time and time again I was found unchanged in my crib, malnourished, and in dirty living conditions. Thankfully, my aunt and uncle helped to feed and clean me up. Aunt Luba would later tell me that she was amazed at how through it all, I would sit in the crib as a hungry and dirty baby, but often content and quiet. However, even my attitude of perspective, contentment, and seeing the bright side was shattered by a few words from Aunt Luba at the airport. Excited to share my faith with my biological father, I was ready to go see him and share the good news of what a relationship with Jesus looks like. With sadness, Aunt Luba told me that my biological father, Gena, had died three months before my arrival. On February 1, 2009, he was crossing the street drunk, was hit by a car, and pronounced dead shortly after. He was 70 years old. After hearing this, my faith was truly shaken. I had thoughts of *why would God allow for this to happen, or why would He give me a passion to share my faith, only to come up short?* During the next few weeks of my visit to Russia, as I visited the orphanage I grew up in from the age of five to ten, I wrestled a lot with these thoughts of letdown as well as the great sadness that came out of seeing the orphanage and the neighborhood I grew up in. *Is God really in control? Are my beliefs real? Is God real?*

This sadness and these moments of uncertainty in my faith at the age of seventeen were due in part to the fact that I had been a Christian for only five years. Yet, the other part of wrestling with my faith came from the innate Russian pride and stubbornness that caused me to not accept Christ in my heart until I turned twelve. This pride was a daily wrestle of surrendering the lordship of my life over to God. So, learning of my biological father's passing months before arriving on my "mission" to share my faith with him only added to the struggle of surrendering my life to the lordship of Jesus Christ. *Why would God give me a desire to share my faith, only to come up just short of my goal? Was my faith too new and I didn't fully understand what I had gotten myself into?*

However, as I talked with my mom, she reminded me of the possibility of my biological father meeting another Christian who may have shared the good news of the Gospel with him. In turn, I live with the hope of seeing him one day in heaven. Faith tested through the fire has allowed me to know God more personally. The fire has also refined my understanding in that it is not the person who shares the Gospel who saves, but only Jesus. It is a privilege to be used by God as seed planters of the faith, but simply remarkable to watch God water the soil of others' faith. As for salvation and accepting Jesus as my Savior, the hope was found for me in Romans 10:9-13, "That if you confess with your mouth, 'Jesus is Lord,' and believe in your heart that God raised him from the dead, you will be saved. For it is with your heart that you believe and are justified, and it is with your mouth that you confess and are saved. As the Scripture says, 'Anyone who trusts in him will never be put to shame.' For there is no difference between Jew and Gentile—the same Lord is Lord of all and richly blesses all who call on Him, for 'everyone who calls on the name of the Lord will be saved.'" I may not have been able to share the Gospel and the message of salvation with my biological dad, but I know that I am not the Savior. Who or what are you trying to save? Are you trying to be the Savior? Good news—you don't have to be. You can let go. Are you currently asking "*Is God really in control? Are my beliefs real? Is God real?*" Good news—God is here for you as He was there for me in the darkest of times.

Valleys can also be a place of hope, finding your encouragement, or community.

I was homeschooled from fifth grade through senior year of high school. In addition to a science group and a theater group, I played homeschool sports. One of those smaller valley moments that led to me finding hope, inspiration and encouragement was during my sophomore year, playing basketball for the Washington County Homeschool Association's (WCHSA) Royal Eagles. I had started a game early in the season poorly, air-balling four straight shots. I figured that my time on the court that game would be over and my starting spot for the season would be gone. However, at halftime, my coach (Coach

G.) came to me, put his hands on my shoulders and looked me in the eye. He said, "Vanya, you are my shooter. Keep shooting. I believe in you." Who would have thought that that moment in 2009 would have stuck with me to this day? I have reflected on that moment often and am so thankful that a coach cared enough to speak encouragement, life, and purpose into me. Though in a seemingly insignificant basketball game, that has become a key moment in how I approach situations and look to be Coach G. to those around me. How can you be an encourager to yourself, or to someone around you and speak life and purpose in the major and seemingly insignificant moments? Ohh yes, I did come out of halftime as a starter, executed the good ole Wisconsin Swing Offense, and hit my first four shots. Did those shots change my life? They did not. However, the words of life behind those shots certainly did.

Keep Flying the Plane

Growing up, through the age of twenty-five, it was a goal of mine to save my heart for the woman I would one day marry. Through high school and college, there were opportunities to date, but with every prayer and possible open door, I did not feel at peace about pursuing a relationship. After graduating from UW-Green Bay at the age of twenty-three, that mindset of saving my heart for a special woman remained. Yet, a door was beginning to open with what you may call the strangest set of events. In the fall of 2013, a week before I was set to start my junior year of college, my 1996 Pontiac Sunfire broke down. Being without a car for the first month of college was challenging in a few ways. Whether it was a drive to the grocery store or attending church on Sundays, I had to rely on friends to get around. Thankfully, my good friend Gabe was not only willing to drive me around but introduced me to Spring Lake Church. I would attend Spring Lake Church from September of 2013 to this day. I joined the worship team in the fall of 2015, shortly after graduating college. Two years later I started dating a woman from Spring Lake.

As we dated, we were amazed at how God used my car breaking down and the return of her family to Spring Lake for us to meet. However, the dates became more spaced out and quality time began to fade as I embarked on my second campaign for the Green Bay City Council. The lack of quality time together would eventually lead to my girlfriend breaking up with me, three days before the April 3, 2018, election. Three days later I lost the election by fifty-nine votes. This was a challenging time, but things began to look up when a few months later, my girlfriend and I got back together and were engaged on our one-year anniversary. With eight months of engagement under our belt and only 150 days before the wedding, my fiancée unexpectedly called off our engagement.

The news of a broken engagement brought about the most painful days I have ever experienced. The sorrow, betrayal, and the unlove that I felt were overwhelming. For someone who normally can hold their emotions pretty well, for the first few months after the broken engagement, I struggled to do so. For instance, I would be in the kitchen making a sandwich, or brushing my teeth before bed, when a deep and overwhelming sadness would envelop me. I would break down in tears two to three times a day. In these challenging moments, I knew that hundreds of friends and family members were praying for me. In addition to feeling the support of those prayers, I would call and talk to close friends. There were many amazing conversations that I could write a separate book about. My family and friends rallied around me to the point of two of my best friends letting me live with them for a few months while I sorted things out. My purpose was hard to see, much less live out in this valley. Still, there was a particular conversation with a friend who was a pilot and had a knack for aviation. This friend said that while he did not have all the answers as to why God was putting me through this trying time, he did say that like a pilot in distress, I had to keep flying the plane. He went on to explain that most plane crashes are preventable, but happen because the pilot does not rely on their training and gives up on flying the plane. My friend reminded me that my training was in the Word of God—the Bible. At that moment I was reminded of my life verse found in Philippians 2:13. I could feel God's calming presence reassure my soul with the words of that scripture: "For it is God who works in you to will and to act according to His good purpose."

So, while I did not understand or have all the answers, I knew that if I obeyed God and left all consequences to Him, then all that took place was for my good.

That is a part of God's purpose. I chose to live out my purpose even in this dark season. The purpose may not have been to help others, but rather recharge and receive help from family and friends. I thank those who lived out their purpose and loved me when I needed it most. Further, Philippians 2:13 is a reminder that God works out all things for our best—even when we are not at our best—for our ultimate good and His omniscient (all knowing) purpose.

As I chose to daily fly the plane, or live my life with positivity and purpose, God backfilled His blessings. One of those blessings amid my great sadness was an email from my alma mater UW-Milwaukee at Washington County notifying me of being named their alumnus of the year, only six years after graduating with my associate degree. In my words of thanks, I was able to share that success also comes with living the painful moments of life. I went on to share the challenges I had with losing two elections and a broken engagement. As I did six years earlier in my commencement address to the graduating class of 2013, I encouraged the graduates by saying we have a choice to stay in a corner swallowed up in our pain and sadness, or we can get up and find someone in a corner and extend our hand to help. I again chose to live out my purpose in this season.

Finally, little did I know that our God of healing and restoration would allow me to meet my now wife, Callee, in July of 2021 at Lifest, a Christian music festival in Oshkosh, Wisconsin. I will share more in a chapter to come, but as the Good Book says, "Weeping may endure for a night, but joy comes in the morning." (Psalm

30:5b). Callee is an amazing blessing to me. Despite the challenges of the past, God certainly had the very best in mind for me. God has the very best in mind for you too. Whether in singleness, a broken relationship, or a thriving marriage,

God sees you and is ready to give you His very best—in His timing (Philippians 2:13),

if you are willing to surrender yourself to Him. As I read my vows to Callee on our wedding day, I chose to live out my purpose of loving God and people once more and made this loving covenant (agreement) with Callee: "Callee, I promised to not start these vows with the phrase 'My fellow Americans,' so I won't. Dear Callee Marie, soon-to-be Koepke, what an incredible journey that only our detail-oriented God could take us on. From the seemingly impossible odds of meeting while growing up 5,515 miles apart as kids, 30 minutes apart on Hwy 33 as teens, to a year of failed attempts of a blind date in our twenties, God used every second to bring us closer to each other at the most perfect time. From our first handshake and hello at Lifest, to our first date at Cozumel Mexican restaurant, to today's 'I do,' I am so thankful that you are a part of my life, and I love you as much as only a Russian can love. Truly though, I love you with all that I am and ask God to help me love you more fully each day. I want to have a 1 Corinthians 13 kind of love for you. In advance, I ask for your patience with my stubbornness and grace when I am not the best me that you deserve. I once heard a story about a man who wrote a Valentine's card to his wife saying that he loved her and that she was his whole world. With love, the woman responded that she could never be his whole world, as only Jesus could be that. So, like this story, while I cannot be your whole world as I am only a sinful human redeemed hourly by God's grace, still, I resolve to give you my best love, care, support, and admiration as we seek God together. I pray that the foundation of our faith and a union of you, me, and God will be refined daily to look more like the Trinity of God, Jesus, and the Holy Spirit. In this relationship, no one is higher, but the message of Ephesians 5 is lived out, where we submit to each other out of reverence for Christ. Callee, I resolve to love, protect, cherish, and lead you closer to Jesus. I resolve to provide, lead our home spiritually, and not make all the decorating decisions. I resolve not to go to bed angry but to hold your hand and prayerfully close each day with you. I resolve to value your opinion and feedback above personal, political, or career goals. We are a team, and each decision will be made as such. As you know, ever since we saw a dog in a Starbucks drive-through getting a puppuccino, we call anything cute a 'puppuccino.' So, a reminder that you will always be my 'puppuccino.' Callee, I love you and look forward to spending the rest of my life here on earth and eternity in heaven with you."

Where Is God When Things Are Hopeless?

I have often been told how wonderfully my life was transformed after I accepted Jesus as my Lord and Savior, ideas of "Look at how good things are now," "Looks like you were in the valley and are now on the mountain top." While to an extent, there is truth and consolation in these ideas, the fact of the matter is that after being adopted and accepting Jesus as my Lord and Savior, the hard things of life still happen. Life challenges happen through smaller disappointments, such as a failed first driver's test on September 2, 2009. The disappointments rise through lost city council races at the age of 23 (2016) and 25 (2018). And soul-crushing disappointments such as a broken engagement, 150 days before the wedding.

With these things considered, others may be asking, "Where is this wonderful transformation in your life?" "Where is God when things are hopeless?" At this point I must pause and reflect on the idea of a faith-filled life and its correlation to a pain-free life.

Faith and a relationship with God do not promise a pain-free life. The Bible does not promise an easy life once we accept Jesus in our hearts, but it does promise that He will be with us and give us a supporting community with whom to work through challenges. John 16:33 reminds us, "I have told you these things, so that in me you may have peace. In this world you will have trouble. But take heart! I have overcome the world." In turn, we should not give up on our purpose-driven life when things get tough. Like weightlifting, where we force our muscles to tear slightly and rebuild, we have to go through hard and challenging situations to gain strength for what may lie ahead. Whether that strength is for us, or to be a loving, caring, and a relational presence for someone else going through what we may have gone through, the purpose of the pain is never in vain. Life can be hard at times and does require hard work. However, you may actually be strengthening your muscle memory for your next valley or a valley of another who will need you.

Some may say, "Well, Vanya, haven't you arrived? You've overcome your challenges and written a book about it—you're an author!" While there is some truth to this (I did write a book), I am far from arriving and will not fully arrive until I am face-to-face with God. Until then, my story and your story are not over. There will be more valleys and mountain top moments. I am ready to embrace whatever may come by the grace of God. In some moments it may be easy to live out a purposeful life to the fullest, while others may seem impossible. However, as I reflect on my story, look at your story and

tell those lies of "impossible" to go away— know that you are an overcomer.

When I reflect on my story, here is what it looks like. If my biological dad had died on the submarine, I would not be here today. If my extended family and neighbors did not feed and take care of me, I may not be here today. If the orphanage did not provide for me (yes, see the blessing and provision in not ideal circumstances), or teach me the value of hard work, I would not be who I am today. In fact, I remember doing orphanage chores like washing three flights of concrete stairs on hands and knees—it was a nasty job (think spit, dirt, and cigarette butts). Between the ages of five and ten, I remember my chore of potato peeling at the orphanage as well. I would be given a tub of potatoes, a regular cutting knife (no peelers) and would work on peeling potatoes for a few hours. To this day, I enjoy peeling potatoes, but with the luxury of an American potato peeler!

Growing up in Wisconsin and being homeschooled further instilled the values of discipline and hard work. I worked on many remodeling, construction, painting, and landscaping jobs through high school. When I attended college at UW-Washington County (now UWM-Washington County), I worked concessions, at the student union, and officiated intramural sports. During the summers, I worked as a landscaper at a condo complex in Germantown. The first summer was a bucket and gloves to pull weeds all day. The second summer, I helped trim bushes and pick weeds, and the third summer I had graduated to grooming the lawn with beautiful lines on my zero-turn mower. At UW-Green Bay, I had three part time jobs in combinations ranging from the following: operating a camera at sporting events, working as a resident assistant, a teaching assistant, an intramural official, and serving as the Student Government President. Homework was typically done between 10 p.m. and 2 a.m. There were many all-nighters as well (as in academic and not party all-nighters, that is). During my junior year at UW-Green Bay, I also had a paid internship with the City of De Pere Planning and Zoning Department that taught me many great skills. However, another challenge came up when I was declined for my senior year internship with the Village of Bellevue and the Village of Allouez. I again felt rejected and was worried about not getting the experience and the pay that came with the internship during winter break. Still, thanks to the help of a few professors, I received an internship with the Green Bay Mayor's Office about a month later. It's simply amazing how things come together after what seems like a rejection, challenge, or failure.

Now in my career, in elected office, high-school basketball officiating, worship team volunteering (playing piano at my church), and most importantly, my marriage, the hard work continues. I do not say all these things to have your purpose be hard work. Hard work helps but is not everything. Rather, I tell you these things to remind you that I am just a person who had to dig deep and develop the skill to be an overcomer and to rely on God during those seasons. I am not some lofty author who has it all together or had an easy past. Instead, I am a person who was blessed by God, blessed with a strong community, and was equipped to share some advice with you. My hope is that we can lock arms, and as you do a similar overview of your story (that may be entirely different than mine), build a spirit of overcoming, rely on God and community, and that you too can better mold yourself into living out your purpose.

Similar to when my parents encouraged me to officiate basketball during my sophomore year of high school in 2009 because they wanted me to see the game from all angles (since I was already a player and a coach), think of how you can see your situations from all sides. Circumstances only seem hopeless from one perspective. When you see all sides of the situation, you will see hope and the coming expiration date of your trials.

In all, when we wonder where God is when things seem hopeless, He is there for us—whether we have trusted Him or not. He may manifest Himself through a person who is there for us, like my Aunt Luba, or through an answered prayer that should pull us closer to God. Challenges can either pull us closer to God and help us understand His presence in our seemingly helpless situations, or push us further from God. The beautiful thing is that the choice is ours. In either situation, do not underestimate the opportunity to be the person God uses as an answer to someone's prayer. Instead of sitting in a corner and pouting about a challenging situation, choose to get up, find a corner with someone else in it, extend a helping hand, and lift them out of the corner.

Hopeless situations are a corner and are an extended hand away from becoming a renewed purpose and a genuine relationship.

Vanya's biological father Genadevich Alexsandrovich Bezhenzev.

In addition to the submarine, this was one of the ships that Vanya's father served on while in the Russian navy Pacific Fleet. Vanya's grandpa Alexander also served in WWII from June 22nd, 1941 until the end.

On the far right (man with beard) is Vanya's great-grandpa who he was named after (father of Vanya's grandma Poluferia). Vanya's great-grandpa, Ivan Makeev, was a cabinet maker and known as the master of all trades.

Vanya's child hood home at 17 Slavyanskiy Pereulok (Slavic Lane).

Vanya with Kevin and Liz Gallagher at the age of eight in Long Island, NY.

Vanya in New York at the age of eight with the Twin Towers in the
background July of 2000.

Vanya, his dad Paul, older brother Tyler and mom Dawn in their first picture together at the Russian orphanage.

Vanya and Galina with their parents Paul and Dawn Koepke in front of Tomsk Univeristy during their second trip to Russia (when they finished the adoption).

Vanya having tea in Russia with his Aunt Luba,
Uncle Vitya, and cousin Nadya.

Vanya's Russian and American family pictures as well as his Green Bay
Police & Fire Commissioner badge and the 15 under 40 award.

Vanya's ring from his Russian family as well as a carved painting from his birth city Tomsk.

Vanya and Callee on their wedding day (Nov. 18th, 2022) in front of Lambeau Field in Green Bay, WI.

Vanya in Spain at the age of six. Similarly to his biological dad, the host family raised pigeons.

Vanya at the age of five with his Russian cousins and extended family.

The orphanage where Vanya lived between ages five and ten.

Vanya's biological dad's Russian navy ring as well as pictures of his
biological Dad, Grandma Poluferia, his Aunt Luba and Uncle Vitya on
the far right.

Channeling Pain to Purpose

How does one find purpose amidst the regular pain of life? In short, purpose is found through choosing to channel our pain into a positive purpose. After all, when life strikes with its pain and challenges, we tend to run towards entertainment, drinking, and anything that brings us pleasure and temporarily reduces the pain of reality. Will another weekend or a vacation ease the pain and fill the void? Are you just living for the weekend? Now, we all need a break from time to time, but the challenge lies in not letting those "breaks" consume us and hold us back from our purpose. For instance, there is nothing wrong with entertainment, reading a book, or watching a movie. In fact, I am the first to watch good movies like *Star Wars, Lord of the Rings, Remember the Titans,* or the occasional chick-flick. However, when we allow our enjoyment of entertainment to become a worship of celebrities, authors, and actors, it leads to a severe delay in our contribution to the world, one that ultimately leads to feeling purposeless and unfulfilled. This is the case as we allow the lives of others to dictate our limited days in this world. Foregoing reading a gossip magazine on a daily basis may allow you time to write a life-changing blog or a book. A more disciplined approach to binge-watching shows may give you time to visit a senior home and invest in the lives of those who do not have anyone investing in them.

Some may say that the above steps are too radical and unnecessary, yet in reality, given the limited amount of time we have on this earth to live out our purpose, we simply have to prioritize our time; even if it means changing our habits to make more time for living out our purpose. Purpose through everyday and seemingly small things is just as important. In his book *Atomic Habits*, James Clear shares practical advice on small daily changes that lead to new positive habits over time: "Every action you take is a vote for the person you wish to become." He further adds, "Your habits shape your identity, and your identity shapes your habits." When we approach change in our life, we must start small. Maybe it's 20 minutes less on social media, two fewer negative songs or podcasts, or one less negative friend who puts us into compromising situations.

Change is possible when you view life not as what others have not done or have not been for you, but rather view life as what you will do and will be for others.

We must choose daily to live with this mindset. This approach will revert our thinking of collapsing during challenging times to blossoming and channeling pain into purpose.

What if we took the time to encourage one another? What if we didn't rely on the encouragement of a Dove Chocolate or a fortune cookie, but spoke words of life into one another? What if we took a few minutes to build up another person with words or deeds more powerful than the hours spent pursuing temporary happiness? The answer is simple: with words of encouragement we will stir, awaken, and re-energize a life of purpose in one another; a life that is worth living.

> *"Therefore encourage one another and build each other up."*
> **1 Thessalonians 5:11a.**

In order to fully channel pain into purpose, we have to know our foundation. We have to know our source of truth. As you have read in this book so far, I contend that the foundation and source of truth should be one built on a personal relationship with Jesus Christ. However, it is important to note that faith, church, God, and Jesus-followers may be the very reason for pain, disappointment, and a lack of purpose in your life today. If you have been hurt or betrayed by people in the church, the church staff, or people who claimed to be Jesus' followers, I am so sorry. Note that there are wolves in sheep's clothing who will reap ultimate justice from God Himself. Unfortunately, it is the people who claim to be Christians who are often the ones who put a black eye on the face of Christ. While only God is perfect and people fail, God is never the one who causes the pain directly if done at the hand of a Christian. Whether intentional or unintentional, Christians who fail to exemplify a forgiving and a loving God have not fully repented of their sins and are simply bad people who are lying to themselves. In fact, I am sure that there are instances where I have not lived up to fully being a Christian to those around me. For those instances, I too am sorry and pray each day that God would help me to be less of me and more of Him. I have strong convictions and won't change that, but I always strive to give hope and purpose to those around me. Further, in what may be contrary to our culture today, we must choose to not use differences to attack the personality or credibility of another person. What is a more caring and counter-cultural way to resolve these differences?

In turn, despite the weaknesses in a Christian, there is no weakness in the foundation of Christ Himself. Some people may ignore this foundation because they were hurt by the faith community, some may not have this foundation because they were never exposed to it, and some choose to leave this foundation of Jesus Christ because it is different from what their parents believe. I would like to address the latter. If we do not make our faith our own in how we live, treat those around us, and surrender our lives to God, we may more easily choose the faith of our friend, teacher, or professor. However, just because someone chooses a foundation of their friend, teacher, or professor, it does not make that foundation better than that of their parents, but instead it becomes the foundation of another person rather than that of their parents. Why do so many kids walk away from their Christian faith in college? Most likely it is due to them not making a faith their own or being hurt by someone who claimed to be of that faith group. God leaves the choice to each person and gives us all free will though. In turn, channeling pain into purpose may look different for each one of us. I would encourage you to build or rebuild that foundation through a relationship with Jesus Christ. My prayer for you is that you would be that better light than someone who failed you in the church. My prayer would be that you would not live in resentment, brokenness, nor in a faith "different than your parents," but in a life of surrender to Christ and His firm foundation. What do these steps look like? They are fairly simple. As you would in any relationship, spend time with God by reading the Bible and talking with Him in prayer. Find a trustworthy Christian mentor (this may take time if you were failed by someone before), check out a Bible-preaching church online, and eventually connect with the church by attending and joining a small group. Know that God will redeem your past, hold those who failed you accountable, and help you channel your pain into an incredible purpose.

> *"Do your best to present yourself to God as one approved, a worker who does not need to be ashamed and who correctly handles the word of truth."*

2 Timothy 2:15

In some cases, channeling pain into purpose may require a revival of the heart. When I think of a revival, I think of Billy Graham and his famous crusades that led to the salvation of over a million people. These crusades had a simple message of our brokenness and the need for a healer—Jesus Christ, who died for our sins. In Graham's six decades of ministry from the late '40s until the early 2000s, it is amazing how many people heard this simple message, responded to the spirit moving within them, and chose to turn their lives in a new direction— they repented. While revivals are not as popular as they used to be, or go viral like TikTok videos, something interesting happened in February of 2023. As I write this book, a prayer service at Asbury College, in Willmore, Kentucky, has not stopped and has formed into a revival. Thousands of people came to this small college and a town of four thousand people to find hope, a revival, and to channel their pain into a purpose. The official dates for the Asbury revival were February 8th-February 24th, when the twenty-hour prayer and worship services were moved off campus due to logistical issues. However, the revival is staying viral and spreading to other churches and campuses. A hunger for truth, life, and genuine love is being fed through these revivals. Further, a revival of the heart does not require travel and can start in you right where you are reading this book. A revival doesn't have to be a temporary feeling, but can be that turning point in your life where you accept the hope and forgiveness of Jesus and choose to channel pain into a purpose in your life. What was your last revival? Did the last weekend and vacation not do it? What will be your permanent revival today?

The Final Destination

My wife Callee and I were married on November 18th, 2022; it was an amazing day. The months of celebrating the engagement, doing wedding planning, and settling into our home together were purposeful and intentional. However, saying "I do" on November 18th was not the final destination of our marriage or life. If the wedding day was our final destination, we would be in serious trouble. As you may know or have experienced, marriage takes a lot of work. As Callee and I communicate, care for each other, and balance our schedules to make each other a priority, we are finding ways in which our marriage can succeed not merely by our efforts, but on a foundation of Jesus Christ and through intentionality. Callee and I didn't just want to get married for fun, but wanted to have a purposeful marriage that changes the people and the world around us for the better. We desire to live out our life together purposefully, rooted in action and in love while glorifying our Lord and Savior Jesus.

As you seek your purpose, or perhaps are looking to rekindle your passion toward a refocused purpose, have you thought of the end game? What is your ultimate goal in living out and filling out the purpose in life? Is it social status? Is it an income level? A relationship? A material possession? Or what do you believe happens after your time here on earth—the ultimate end game? Unfortunately, I have seen a lack of complete satisfaction and contentment in people who limit themselves to these material goals. I have seen the cycles of hurrying through work days, work months, and years only to find the retirees hungry to work and live out a purpose driven life. Have you ever thought why many retired individuals volunteer, get a part-time job, or meticulously trim their lawns? I believe the answer lies in the fact that retirement is not the final destination either. Now, is this because retired individuals do not enjoy relaxing, warm places, vacations, or crossing items off the bucket list? Not at all. There are wonderful things to look forward to in retirement, but as you may have noticed, even retired people are looking for a board to serve on, a grandchild to watch, or an organization for which to volunteer — those people are looking for their new purpose, in a new season of life. Still, retirement is not the totality of finding and living out our purpose. No matter the stage of life, let's aim for purpose over aimless pleasure. C.S. Lewis writes about the downfalls of being too easily pleased: "It would seem that Our Lord finds our desires not too strong, but too weak. We are half-hearted creatures, fooling about with drink and sex and ambition when infinite joy is offered to us, like an ignorant child who wants to go on making mud pies in a slum because he cannot imagine what is meant by the offer of a holiday at the sea. We are too easily pleased."

As we weigh successes and challenges, God must be our center, identity, and purpose. Because of this, living our life and working in excellence is key to reaching our final destination. Our purpose must be a verb (it has to do something) and found in love (a selfless love). Bob Goff's book *Love Does* is an excellent reminder of how to do this. Goff writes, "Maybe God is doing some inexplicable things in your life. Each of us gets to decide every time whether to lean in or step back—to say yes, ignore it, or tell God why He has the wrong person." Goff further adds, "[We] get the invitation every morning when [we] wake up to actually live a life of complete engagement, a life of whimsy, a life where love does."

Some of us may not be aware of our goals, or the final destination after high school, college, career, retirement, or after death. This may be the case for a few reasons. One, we are struggling to earn acceptance, rather than living out our unique purpose. Two, we are all about the latest hottest thing and just blend in by copying those around us. Three, we are distracted by technology and fail to invest in genuine relationships. Let's examine each area a bit closer. After all, if we are aware of the weaknesses in our life, we can better recalculate how to live out our purpose and be secure in our final destination.

Just like the eight-year-old me, many of us are struggling to earn acceptance and are trying to get by, through being fake, mean, or bitter. In other and more unique situations, some of us may feel trapped in an abusive relationship, drugs, or seemingly unbeatable addictions to alcohol or pornography. However, it does not have to be this way when you choose to say no to these areas of pain, surround yourself with a life-building community that holds you accountable, and ultimately have your purpose and identity wrapped up in Jesus.

The second area is that of copying those around us and a push for instant gratification (when you need that car, house, or thing just like your neighbor right now), and hiding our insecurities in others' well-covered messes. Often, what our neighbors or friends have, we cannot afford (and perhaps nor can they), or simply do not belong in our lives. People take on debt, sacrifice family time, and make choices that only pull them further away from their purpose and their ultimate destination. Even if it is the good things you see from friends, family, or a coworker, it does not mean you have to copy them exactly—be the unique you—be secure in your purpose, identity, and relationships.

The third area is that of our distracted mind, soul, and heart. Have you thought of what your purpose could be in relationship to those around you simply by making intentional eye contact? What conversations could be sparked, what encouragement could you bring through a simple smile and a hello? Yes, let's humanize one another again. Let's maximize in-person relationships and not solely rely on technology and social media to build meaningful relationships. Say "Hi" to the passerby on the sidewalk, a coworker in a hallway, or a classmate on the way to class. When we are secure in our purpose and know our final destination, we will not hide our insecurities behind our ingenuousness, our sin, or the insecurities of others. Yes, let's use technology as needed (a wonderful tool), but not hide behind its filters. Let's choose to be real.

So, as you approach each day, each interaction, how are you stepping up to the plate, setting aside the distractions and unnecessary pleasures to live with the final destination in mind?

Discipline, Decisions, and Forgiveness That Lead to Your Purpose

As I write this book, I think about the necessity to stay disciplined and focused to finish it. In the same vein, my encouragement to you in this chapter is that in order to live out your purpose, discipline is key. After all, from our childhood, there is discipline for breaking the rules, there is a penalty in sports. In college too the fields of academia are often categorized as disciplines. You may be wondering, *"Why have I not found my purpose?"* Most of the time, the answer lies in a lack of discipline.

Whether it is in writing, school, work, or relationships, each area of your life requires a level of discipline in order to live out your very best purpose. You may start small. What does the start to your day look like? Do you roll over, scroll through social media and emails on your phone? Or do you have a disciplined routine of exercise, packing a meal, or an encouraging devotional read? As I mentioned earlier, even if you improve your start of day, mid-day and end of day by just one percent per week, you'll be fifty-two percent better in a year! Ultimately, what matters are the inputs that you allow to drive your day when you wake up. Feeling anxious, depressed, and lonely? Then perhaps scrolling through depressing news, the perfectly filtered social media posts, and listening to music that does not encourage or motivate you are all areas that need change and discipline.

Once you start implementing discipline into the various areas of your life, you may still be asking, *"How do I decide on what is next to fulfill my purpose?"* This is a good question. I believe that the next two areas that will impact your life and set you on the trajectory of your purpose are the areas of decision-making and forgiveness. Let's explore decisions first.

Decisions, whether big or small, can be life-altering; that is why we all wish we had a decision-making guide. While each decision in your life will be unique, there are five principles given by Dr. Charles Stanley that can serve as that very decision-making guide. These principles are: Consulting the Bible, Exercising Wisdom, Praying (and asking for God's and not our will), Godly Counsel, and Following the Holy Spirit. Now, if you are not yet a believer, not all five principles will benefit you. However, consider the applicable ones and how all five may possibly change your life. If you are a believer, how can you fully embrace all five? Let's dive in and discover what each one may mean for things as small as a vacation or as big as a new job or a new relationship.

The first principle revolves around consulting the Word of God, the Bible. Nothing fancy about it, if you have a relationship with God it's a great place to start. If not, it is still a great place to start also and get to know God as well as what He promises us.

The second principle is to exercise wisdom. We've all been given a brain as well as experiences to know how to apply wisdom, or at least weigh things in our life a certain way. As Dr. Charles Stanley likes to say, "Obey God and leave all consequences to Him." This thought is so true, as it applies to both spiritual and non-spiritual applications. If you consider a choice, consider the consequences, good or bad, that go along with that choice.

The third principle is to pray and ask God for His will. This is kind of interesting, as we normally hear or are told to just pray. But what Dr. Charles Stanley is getting at is that prayer should always be coupled with the foundation of asking for God's will. How often do we pray for things that we want or need? How often do we lay out our desires, anxieties, and fears to God? Now, while all these things are part of prayer (we should bring anything to God, the praises and the sorrows), yet at the same time, we have to go outside our wisdom, our understanding and our desires and ask for God's perspective. We must surrender and let God know that we accept the timing for the answer to our prayer, whether it is today, tomorrow, two months or two years from now. Can we pray with the expectation that God's will, guidance, and wisdom be done in our lives? I recall that when I specifically prayed for God's will and timing to be done in my future relationship, after the broken engagement, He led me to Callee. Though I thought I could never trust, be vulnerable, or pursue a relationship for decades, God had other plans. Isaiah 55:8-9 reads: "'For my thoughts are not your thoughts, neither are your ways my ways,' declares the Lord. 'As the heavens are higher than the earth, so are my ways higher than your ways, and my thoughts than your thoughts.'"

The fourth principle is godly counsel. I am so thankful for the godly counsel of my pastors, a few close friends, parents and grandparents over the years. Don't be afraid to reach out for that godly counsel—be in community—do not fly the plane solo. Text or call them and reflect on your situation, reflect on the direction you are leaning towards through prayer, and get their perspective on your situation and which decision you should make. Now, there is a fine line here. Don't just make all your decisions solely based on advice from those around you, even if it is from a trusted or a godly friend. Just because your pastor or a friend says something does not make it the will of God. You should always weigh your decisions with all five of the principles combined.

The fifth principle is that of following the Holy Spirit. This is kind of an interesting idea, especially coming from the Baptist pastor, Dr. Charles Stanley who is, let's just say, not the most Pentecostal pastor out there. However, this an important principle no matter your denomination. The Bible talks about those who accept Christ as their personal Savior and repent of their sins as being filled with the Holy Spirit (yes, God dwells in us). 2 Corinthians 3:17 says, "Now the Lord is the Spirit, and where the Spirit of the Lord is, there is freedom." The Holy Spirit is capable of transforming our hearts of stone, melting away our pain, and putting away the past to a renewed future with Christ. When we live a life of repentance, we live a life of union with the Holy Spirit, and His promptings will only solidify our decisions when applied to these five principles. When we are led by the Holy Spirit, we are led by a Holy God who is omniscient (all knowing), who is omnibenevolent (all good) and omnipotent (all powerful). Proverbs 11 is a great chapter when it comes to wise decision-making. Specifically read verses 2-8, 11-13, 20, 23 and 30.

"When pride comes, then comes disgrace,
but with humility comes wisdom."
Proverbs 11:2

"The fruit of the righteous is a tree of life,
and the one who is wise saves lives."
Proverbs 11:30

In addition to scripture, and Dr. Charles Stanley, author Carole Hildebrand gives the following advice on decisions: "Most of us have weak decision-making muscles. We do not realize what it means to make a real decision. We fail to recognize the force of change that a truly congruent, committed decision makes." Carole adds, "The word 'decision' comes from Latin roots, with *de* meaning 'down' or 'away from' and *caedere* meaning 'to cut.' Therefore, a decision means cutting yourself off from any other possibility." Lastly, Carole states that, "Committed decisions show up in two places: your calendar and your bank account. No matter what you say you value, or even think your priorities are, you have only to look at last year's calendar and bank account to see the decisions you have made about what you truly value."

Now, just because I am writing these things down in this book does not mean I have attained and mastered all of them. I too, like you, am working to get one percent better each day and am relying on the grace of God to see me through.

Remember, God does not bless us for our right actions, but rather blesses the response represented by those actions.

And that response should be rooted in the purposeful pursuit of His holiness. Further, our pursuit of God's holiness is not for the sake of earning our salvation (as Jesus has done all the work by dying on the cross and rising from death), but through the knowledge and repentance that God has opened a way—a response of conviction that leads to repentance is one found when our knowledge of God and His word flows from our minds to our hearts and transforms us. Lastly, as the lyrics of Casting Crown's song go, "I'm just a nobody, trying to tell everybody, all about Somebody who saved my soul," we should constantly pursue our purpose through humility. Ultimately, it is for the sake of living out our best purpose that is rooted in Christ.

Even if we attain our goals (and not merely by our own efforts), they and we will never be fully complete until we reach the perfection of heaven. Yes, we will rest and be perfect at last, once we pass and leave this world behind.

A disciplined, driven and a decisive approach in what you do are great steps to fully living out your purpose. However, the key ingredient of forgiveness of self and forgiveness of others is a must in order to not seek and attempt to live out your purpose in vain. Did you know that the Bible talks about bitterness and unforgiveness leading to both mental and physical sickness? See Matthew 18:23-35. In addition to the Bible, there is medical evidence for unforgiveness being connected to higher incidence of stress, heart disease, high blood pressure, lowered immune response, anxiety, depression, and other difficulties, according to a Johns Hopkins study.

Let's first discuss the importance of forgiving yourself. We have all made mistakes or let someone down. The selfishness and sin within us tend to do that. Sometimes, we cannot forgive ourselves because the person we hurt won't forgive us. At other times, we believe that we deserve the unending shame, pain, and the negative side effects mentioned above for a lifetime as a form of payment for our mistakes. These thoughts have led to broken families, ended relationships, and at times the ending of one's life. However, such thoughts of failure and unforgiveness are lies. These lies are one of the strongest barriers that can hold someone back from living out their purpose. Whether you do or do not have a personal relationship with Jesus Christ, the concept of unconditional forgiveness may be hard. However, if a perfect, sinless God can take the punishment for our sins on the Cross and choose to forgive us, how much more do sinful and imperfect people owe forgiveness to one another? After all, if we are human, we have all had to ask for forgiveness. If you have asked for forgiveness and were forgiven, embrace that and God's forgiveness. If you have not asked for forgiveness (be sure to do so), or were not forgiven, choose to forgive yourself when you see how the Creator of the world forgave you and the one you may have wronged. God's forgiveness is the ultimate forgiveness. Ephesians 4:32 reminds us, "Be kind to one another, tenderhearted, forgiving one another, as God in Christ forgave you."

Now, let's look at the importance of forgiving others. If we have been forgiven and have chosen to forgive ourselves, we should be the first to forgive those who ask for forgiveness. Mark 11:25 says, "And whenever you stand praying, forgive, if you have anything against anyone, so that your Father also who is in heaven may forgive you your trespasses." I have had to ask for forgiveness and have had to forgive those who hurt me, even when it seemed impossible. Whether it was those who contributed to my difficult childhood, my former fiancée, or others, forgiving them was my first step to mental, spiritual and physical freedom. It's amazing; some believe that unforgiveness is the perfect payback for the hurt caused to them, when in actuality unforgiveness is keeping them trapped. Forgiveness is brutally hard. However, when you consider all who have forgiven you, how can you not forgive those who have hurt you? How can today be the day of forgiveness if you send that text or call of forgiveness? Pause and act right now. Pause and choose to be free. Meditate on Psalm 86:5, "For you, O Lord, are good and forgiving, abounding in steadfast love to all who call upon you."

Ultimately, a purpose-driven life that brings us the satisfaction we desire must be a daily renewal and a disciplined approach in what we listen to, what we read, what we watch, with whom we surround ourselves, and what environments we allow to dictate to us. What are your disciplines? What are your decision-making strategies? Have you forgiven yourself? Have you forgiven those around you—especially those who may have wounded you?

> *"For if you forgive other people when they*
> *sin against you, your heavenly Father will*

also forgive you. But if you do not forgive others their sins, your Father will not forgive your sins. "

Matthew 6:14-15

You should also consider reading Colossians 3. Verses 12-15 specifically stand out: "Therefore, as God's chosen people, holy and dearly loved, clothe yourselves with compassion, kindness, humility, gentleness and patience. Bear with each other and forgive whatever grievances you may have against one another. Forgive as the Lord forgave you. And over all these virtues, put on love, which binds them all together in perfect unity. Let the peace of Christ rule in your hearts, since as members of one body you were called to peace. And be thankful."

Vulnerability

At one point in our lives, the inevitable question arises, "What is the purpose of my life?" Let's explore this question more by reflecting on the block of vulnerability. A leap of faith in a relationship with others and Jesus requires vulnerability. Showing our authentic self through vulnerability leads us to living out our purpose and helping those around us.

As you have seen in the examples from my story, at the heart of our purpose, only Christ can truly satisfy our deepest longing and desire. Nonetheless, what is often missed in this theological explanation is the practical application. This application of living out who we were meant to be rests in vulnerability. I recall the first time I shared my story at the age of ten with my fourth-grade class at Riverside Elementary in Menomonee Falls, WI. More importantly, I recall one of the first times I was fully vulnerable. Within the first few minutes of sharing about my Russian family, I got to the part about the death of my biological mother and broke down in tears. I would not be able to publicly share my story for another five years. Though being vulnerable was painful for me, each time I shared my story thereafter healing took place. Time and time again, my spiritual and personal growth was drawn from vulnerability. Further, when you look at some of your closest relationships, they are most likely based on vulnerability. Know that your healing awaits each time you choose to be vulnerable. Whether it is an inside joke, a shared moment of pain, or a secret, you have a bond with someone due to a shared connection through vulnerability. It is also important to remember that Jesus modeled vulnerability well. Instead of being a distant, disconnected, and an uncaring king on a throne, Jesus was a great model (and THE model) of vulnerability through His empathy and care. In an article entitled, *Jesus Embraced Vulnerability to Unite with the Vulnerable,* Drew Smith states, "Jesus lived a very vulnerable life and was not immune to or protected from challenges that the people of His time confronted every day, especially those persons at the bottom of the embedded social and religious structures." When we consider Jesus' challenging words from His Sermon on the Mount, we see a call to vulnerability woven throughout the scripture. Luke 6:27-31, "But to you who are listening I say: Love your enemies, do good to those who hate you, bless those who curse you, pray for those who mistreat you. If someone slaps you on one cheek, turn to them the other also. If someone takes your coat, do not withhold your shirt from them. Give to everyone who asks you and if anyone takes what belongs to you, do not demand it back. Do to others as you would have them do to you." These words are challenging, but so is vulnerability. Is it worth it, though, based on your closest relationships? Before I continue with deeper insight on how you can live out your purpose more fully through vulnerability and what vulnerability is, it is important to look at what vulnerability is not.

Vulnerability is not a weakness, especially if you are looking to build genuine relationships and to fully live out your purpose (2 Corinthians 12:9). Vulnerability should not be ungenuine, manipulative, or demoralizing. Instead, vulnerability should be seen as the following, based on a TED Talk titled *The Power of Vulnerability,* by Brené Brown. In her TED Talk, Brené says the following about vulnerability: "Connection is why we're here. It's what gives purpose and meaning to our lives." She further adds, "When you ask people about love, they tell you about heartbreak. When you ask people about belonging, they'll tell you their most excruciating experience of being excluded. And when you ask people about connection, the stories they told me were about disconnection." In her further research, Brown discovered that, "Shame is really easily understood as the fear of disconnection: Is there something about me that, if other people know it or see it, that I won't be worthy of connection?" Further, she states, "The thing that underpinned this was excruciating vulnerability. This idea... [that] in order for connection to happen, we have to allow ourselves to be seen, really seen." Further in her research she discovered that, "There was only one variable that separated the people who have a strong sense of love and belonging and the people who really struggle for it. And that was, the people who have a strong sense of love and belonging *believe they're worthy of love and belonging.*" She then took this research, combined the latter and more optimistic groups (who she described as "whole-hearted"), and found that "What they had in common was a sense of courage, compassion, and connection... These folks had the courage to be imperfect. They had the compassion to be kind to themselves first and then to others. They were willing to let go of who they thought they should be in order to be who they were for connection." Further, "The other thing they had in common was they fully embraced vulnerability. They believed what made them vulnerable made them beautiful." Brown continues, "I know that vulnerability is the core of shame and fear, and our struggle for worthiness, but it appears that it's also the birthplace of joy, of creativity, of belonging, of love."

Brown adds, "We live in a vulnerable world, and one of the ways we deal with it is we numb vulnerability. We are the most in debt, obese, addicted, and medicated adult cohort in U.S. history. The problem is that you cannot selectively numb emotion. You can't say, here's the bad stuff, here's vulnerability, here's grief, here's shame, here's fear, here's disappointment. I don't want to feel these. I'm going to have a couple of beers and a banana nut muffin. You can't numb those hard feelings without numbing the other affects, our emotions. You cannot selectively numb. When we numb those, we numb joy, gratitude, happiness, and then we are miserable, and *we are looking for purpose and meaning.* We blame (a way to discharge pain and discomfort and defined by the research community), we perfect, we pretend. There is another way: let ourselves be seen—vulnerably seen. To love with our whole hearts, even though there's no guarantee. To practice gratitude and joy." Have you seen the anxiety, depression, stress, and sickness due to a lack of vulnerability? Have you seen anger on social media, sporting events, or family gatherings, all because someone refuses vulnerability, healing, and love? If you have embraced vulnerability, it does not make you weak or a doormat. Instead, vulnerability makes you the bridge to someone's healing. Don't fight anger with anger, but fight anger, depression, and the pain around you with a story, your story. How can the vulnerability of your story help to heal a broken relationship, or save someone from tragedy?

In turn, what has changed in my life since being ten years old and breaking down at Riverside Elementary while sharing my story? I went from failing to tell my story to sharing it hundreds of times with audiences of one, hundreds, and now writing a book about it. It is simply a vulnerability that developed after I accepted Jesus into my heart as Lord and Savior, because I had at last recognized the vulnerability of the God of the universe and His Son.

After all, prior to being adopted and in the early years of being in America, I was let down and failed so many times that I became bitter, insecure, unthankful, prideful, could not hug people, or even say "I love you." I needed a doctor to break my heart of stone and fill it with love. This moment happened two years after being adopted. When I was twelve my dad was taking my older brother Tyler and me to a church event (AWANA), and while we were driving, I started asking them about Jesus and why He seemed to be what fulfilled their lives, gave them hope and a purpose. I certainly knew that my family was not perfect and had its issues like any other family; however, over the two years since being adopted, I could see how Jesus was the missing puzzle piece in my life that could fill that deep, dark void within me. This void was not even filled with the love and acceptance of my new family (something I had longed for all my life). Simply believing that there was a higher being, being good and pretending to be okay on the outside, while suppressing my pain deep inside was not enough either. I couldn't fool God as He knew my heart fully. I had to go beyond religion and intellectual knowledge of faith to a personal relationship with the Creator of the universe and my heart. Instead, as I was told by my dad on that night as we pulled into a Wal-Mart parking lot on County Line Road Q in Menomonee Falls, that void could only be filled with believing that Jesus had done all the work by dying for my sins, raising from the dead to defeat sin, and letting Jesus sit on the throne of my life. The mask of my life's masquerade, that

I even thought got me adopted, could not last anymore. After further discussion we prayed, and as tears rolled down my face, I confessed my sins, asked God for His help, forgiveness, and asked Jesus to be the Lord of my life. This was and is the defining moment of who I am today. Without the time in that parking lot, the years of prayer for me by my family, and the unconditional grace and mercy of God, my heart of stone may have never been broken. But let me tell you that while in that moment the sky did not open and angels did not come down, I could feel a heavy weight lifted off my heart, I felt refreshed, hopeful, and determined to live my life for the Author of my story. While the building blocks would follow, I had discovered my source of truth and purpose. Since that moment, 18 years have gone by (as I write this book at the age of 30), there have been many ups and downs, successes and failures, heartbreaks and love, but one thing for sure, I know that that prayer was the best decision I have ever made. While I still struggle with pride and overcoming my character flaws and will until I meet Jesus in a perfect heaven where sin does not hold us back from perfection, I know that God and those around me will help mold me into the best version I can be—an imperfect, sinful man, who is redeemed hourly by God's faithful grace.

In part, why Christians struggle to live out their purpose and stumble into hypocrisy, rather than hope and life-change, is due to the lack of vulnerability.

Casting Crowns' song *Stained Glass Masquerade* should challenge us all with its lyrics about hiding our true selves.

You don't have to wait until you are broken to be vulnerable. How can you lead with empathy, find the time and the place to be vulnerable? Better yet, how can you lead in the area of vulnerability—it's not a weakness, but requires humility and a servant leadership approach, an approach that Jesus took when He bore our sins and died on the Cross for each one of them. The Bible is a great resource and has the information needed to equip us with this example of vulnerability. Even Gandhi recognized this: "You Christians look after a document containing enough dynamite to blow all civilization to pieces, turn the world upside down, and bring peace to a battle-torn planet. But you treat it as though it is nothing more than a piece of literature." We must make the most important journey of the Christian faith and live out the foundation of our faith by traveling 12-14 inches from our brains to our hearts. We must live out our purpose on the foundation that can revolutionize the world for the better.

What will our choice be? Will we embrace mercy and grace, or attend the next masquerade?

Mercy: *not receiving the punishment we deserve*

Grace: *receiving the blessings that we don't deserve*

In the end, the relationships we seek and strive to receive, the reciprocation of love and care, begin with vulnerability.

However, the fullest measure of vulnerability can only come through a personal relationship with Jesus Christ. Through this relationship we can truly live out vulnerable and genuine lives, when we fully embrace the fact that Jesus did not die and rise again to start a religion, but rather for us to start a personal relationship with Him. In turn, we will be able to fully embrace our purpose and discover genuine relationships when we are broken, vulnerable and open.

> *"I will give you a new heart and put a new spirit in you; I will remove from you your heart of stone and give you a heart of flesh."*
> **Ezekiel 36:26**

Loneliness

It was the evening of November 26th, 2019, when I recently finished worship team practice at Spring Lake Church. Surprisingly, I had a light schedule that day and the rest of the week, with Thanksgiving only a few days away. As I drove home, a deep feeling of loneliness came over me. I felt tired and worn out from investing in others, volunteering, and keeping busy only to become drained with little reinvestment into me. The only thing that kept the charge going was a text message from my mom the day before saying, "Spending some sweet time with the Lord in prayer for you. Loved a verse I read this morning in Psalms 147:11 that reminds me of you… 'the Lord delights in those that fear Him; who put their hope in His unfailing love.' Have an amazing day! Continue to be a light wherever you go!" These words were extremely powerful, and I fully understood and felt the love in that message. Still, a day later, I felt lonely on this journey of being a light, serving, giving, and feeling little reciprocation to recharge my spiritual and emotional batteries. In addition to feeling unproductive, my Facebook feed was flooded with local political campaign announcements. Of course, the reality of not running for office this year hit that much harder in my moment of loneliness. After all, this was the first time I was not campaigning since my freshman year of college. The successful collegiate student government campaigns between 2011 and 2015 fueled my drive for public service. In turn, the unsuccessful 2016 and 2018 Green Bay City Council campaigns made me just as involved in my community as I was in college. However, knowing that I was not going to be on the ballot in 2020, the feeling of loneliness began to chip away at my drive, focus, and purpose. As I drove, I continued to reflect on factors that were driving this lonely feeling. *Was it the slower week at work? Was it the few basketball games I had to officiate? Was it that my investment in others left me with hundreds of followers, but only a few close friends? Or was it the desire for a dating relationship, now that I was eight months removed from my broken engagement?* As these thoughts circled in my head and the loneliness ate away at the energy in my heart, I broke down in tears. These tears were a desperate plea to God to help me, to encourage me, to give me peace. After making a few unanswered phone calls, I reached out to my friend Alex, who picked up after a few short rings. Through tears, I explained what was going on. For the following 45 minutes, Alex proceeded to give me clarity in my plea for help and encouragement. He reminded me to get back into God's Word—the Bible. He encouraged me to read three separate passages at random and jot down at least three takeaways from each passage. After the phone call that night, Alex's encouragement and God's guidance led me to the following passages and takeaways:

- Psalm 18
    - The Lord was my rock, fortress, and deliverer.
    - The Lord had rescued me because He delighted in me.
    - The Lord would deal with me according to my righteousness; according to the cleanness of my hands, He would reward me.
    - It is God who arms me with strength.
    - The Lord stooped down to make me great.
    - God had delivered me from attacks of people.
    - God avenges me.
- Proverbs 31
    - I do not need to spend my strength on women, but wait on God's match with a woman who clothes herself in strength and dignity.
    - I needed to speak for those who could not speak for themselves.
    - I needed to defend the poor and needy.
- Jeremiah 9
    - Not to boast in anything, unless boasting about how good God is.

- To boast that I know and understand God.

- To make the daily distinction between being judged and held accountable. Judgment leads to an immediate sentence, while accountability leads to immense freedom.

That conversation with a dear friend and the above scriptures were a huge blessing to me that night. In turn, know that it is okay to be sad, lonely, and not always your best. Know that when you go through such moments and seasons you will only come out stronger in the end. Further, especially if you are single or feel like no one is there, know that God is. He has a beautiful purpose for your singleness and will provide a community for you to be encouraged by as long as you allow Him to.

As a Christian, I at times hear, "Well, if you believe in God and if God is real, and if God has changed your life, why do you have struggles?" I simply reply with the promise in the Bible, that while there is a season for everything (Ecclesiastes 3: 1-8), God promises to never leave us or forsake us (Deuteronomy 31:8). God will always give us a way out of challenges; it may be a friend on the phone, a Bible verse, or just crying out to Him in anger and venting.

When we live a life in obedience to Jesus, when our challenges arise, we have a choice to listen to the lies about us that are not true, or to tell that lying voice to shut up.

The devil seeks to kill and destroy through small lies that lead to life-altering decisions. However, Jesus has come to give us a renewed life through a relationship with Him. Jesus can give you a purpose-filled life, a drive, and a way out in difficult situations. It is not always easy and Christianity is not the "easy button," but it truly is worth it.

I would be remiss if I did not encourage a godly counselor or Biblical counseling as additional resources that can help those who cannot seem to get out of a valley and need these professional resources. Even pastors at churches I have attended encouraged seeing a counselor, whether things are good or bad. We are all broken people who should not struggle through life alone. Lean into the truths that God sees in you and loves you for. Lean into a community. But whatever you do, do not do life alone. Know that you are loved and cared for. Music and podcasts are powerful inputs that can alter your days and your mood. This is why 95% of what I listen to is godly music on the radio, or my favorite worship songs on my music streaming service. Don't let your inputs be negative, leading to a garbage in/garbage out mentality.

At the same time, don't pull away from the difficulties of life and insulate yourself from all negativities. Being used by God to encourage someone in a difficult situation is entirely different than choosing to listen to music and watch movies that deflate you. May the lyrics to Matthew West's song *Grace Upon Grace* remind you of your purpose, help you overcome your past mistakes, and truly realize that you are redeemed and made new in God's eyes.

Living Life to the Fullest in All Seasons

The subtitle of this book is *Living Life to the Fullest in All Seasons*. The reason for this title has been summarized in previous chapters, but is worth exploring more closely here. The German philosopher Immanuel Kant once said, "Act in such a way that you treat humanity, whether in your own person or in the person of any other, never merely as a means to an end, but always at the same time as an end."

This quote has been especially important in understanding the actions of my parents in adopting me, my purpose in life, and most importantly, God's plan for your life. In a world full of pain, abuse, fraud, and deceit, genuine love is hard to find. Seemingly, around each corner there is an agenda, or a "What's in it for me?" mentality. People wonder, *"Is this relationship for real?"* *"Is this business transaction based on a relationship or the dollars?"* *"Is this a favor, but with strings attached?"* Or simply, *"What is in it for me?"* Sadly, the opposite of

Kant's and ultimately God's desire for treating one another with genuine care and respect is often true. People tend to use one another as a mode of transportation towards achieving a personal goal, instead of what is best for both parties.

While many instances of genuine relationships have proven to be false, I am fueled by the fact that my relationship with Jesus is not. When Jesus died on the Cross for us all, He did not seek what was in it for Him, but rather, selflessly laid down His life for us. We were not a means to an end, but rather the redemptive end in the selfless sacrifice of Christ. Similarly, I saw my Christian parents adopt and foster out of genuine love that simply reflected the love they received from Christ. In turn, I strive to model the example of Christ and my parents in all my actions. For those who would argue that my testimony is really defined by correlation leading to causation, this is the one time I would concede and say guilty as charged, my parents set a great example for me. Whether pursuing politics in college and working diligently on my internship with the City of De Pere's Planning and Zoning Department, or interning for Green Bay's mayor (Mayor Schmitt, thank you for that awesome foreword), the goal was to do my very best; the goal was to do the best I could out of my appreciation for those working with me. Political favors or preferential treatment were on my radar, but certainly not my motivation. So, when I was appointed to the Green Bay Police and Fire Commission at the age 26, or received support and recognition from those I worked with, I was only driven further to work hard and do my best for those around me. You see, there is nothing wrong with being motivated and having goals. In fact, I have been recognized with awards ranging from UW-Green Bay's Chancellors Leadership Medallion to the 15 under 40 award in Brown County, and an Alumnus of the Year award at UWM-Washington County.

However, be careful not to let your goals, awards and accomplishments become your gods. Such idols end up as dusty plaques on a wall, rather than motivation for dusting off the broken hearts of others that need hope and a purpose.

Do not let your ambition carry you away into a sea of fake friends, fake conversations, and disingenuity that runs through your DNA. Be an inspiration, but never attempt to be the king or queen of your life, as a slice of humble pie awaits. Now, as a husband, an elected official, and a leader at my job, my priority is what is best for all and not just me.

How can you implement a purpose to your home, work, or relationships? While the prior chapters lay a foundation for a purpose-driven life, it is important to note the three Cs. These are: Culture, Connection, and Communication. Without a genuine investment in each, your home, work, and relationships may only be surviving, rather than thriving, in their purpose. In their book *MAGIC*, authors Tracy Maylett and Paul Warner expand on the three Cs I've used in my workplace leading a team, and in my home with my wife. The acronym MAGIC stands for Meaning, Autonomy, Growth, Impact, and Connection. How can you implement these at work, in your home, or classroom? Ultimately, each one points back to purpose and relationships.

As we persevere and make the most of our time on earth with purpose, a reminder from Tim Tebow's book *This is the Day* comes to mind. Tebow writes, "People matter more than schedules, more than lists, and more than tasks. We know this but what does it really mean? How do we live this out? Showing love to others may mean a simple shift in your priorities. Think about what matters most. Choose the more important things over the lesser ones. Balance busy calendars with meaningful moments. Call a friend and let them know you're thinking about them. Unplug the phones, gadgets, and devices, and be more present with a friend, spouse, parent, or child." How are you purposely investing in your relationships?

As we reflect on the prior chapters, it's important to prepare for the application of what was read. Reading these words without application leads to zero change. But how can you be different? As you reflect, compare the diagram that we started with below and fill in your current blocks (more specifically, who or what occupies each block)? Which ones need to change or improve?

Purpose		
Definitions	Preferences	Humility
Vulnerability	Genuine Relationships	Decision-Making
Source of Truth		

Purpose		

In conclusion, life can be defined by our purpose and relationships. What foundation will you choose to build each one on? Our foundation is the source of truth. For me, the source of truth is the Bible, the definitions are the Bible's teachings, and I do my best (and often fail) to make my daily preferences Jesus' preferences. What will your source of truth be? What will your vulnerability, genuine relationships, and decision-making look like? What definitions and preferences will guide you? How will you reflect on your pursuit of purpose through humility? The decision will be up to you; how will the next week, month, and year look different when you consider yourself as a purpose-minded, genuine, community-seeking difference maker? Today is your day. Today is day one.

"The greatest enemy to human souls is the self-righteous spirit which makes men look to themselves for salvation."

Charles Spurgeon